# Table of Contents

# Introduction: The Journey to Starting Your Recording Studio Business

Welcome! You're about to dive into "The Ultimate Guide on How to Start a Recording Studio Business." This book is crafted to walk you through the essential steps and strategies to build a successful recording studio. Whether you're a seasoned professional in the music industry or a complete novice, this guide is packed with insights and knowledge to help you set up and grow your own recording studio.

Starting a recording studio is more than just an exciting venture; it's a way to blend your love for music with entrepreneurship. But be prepared, because running a recording studio demands more than technical prowess. It requires meticulous planning, a deep understanding of your target market, building solid relationships, and delivering top-notch service to stand out in a crowded field.

Throughout this guide, we'll cover a wide range of topics essential for starting and managing a recording studio. Each chapter is filled with valuable information and practical tips to help you navigate challenges and seize opportunities. Let's kick off this journey by laying a strong foundation for your success in the recording studio business.

# Chapter 1: Introduction to the Recording Studio Business

Starting a recording studio business can be an incredibly exciting and rewarding journey. Imagine having a space where music enthusiasts and professionals alike can come together to create, record, and produce high-quality audio content. Whether you already have experience in music production or you're just beginning to explore this field, this chapter is designed to give you a thorough introduction to the recording studio business.

## The Significance of Recording Studios

Recording studios hold a pivotal place in the music industry. They are more than just rooms with fancy equipment; they are creative hubs where artists can bring their musical visions to life. In these controlled environments, equipped with state-of-the-art audio gear and software, artists can ensure their music is captured and produced at the highest possible quality.

Think about it: without recording studios, many of the tracks we love and cherish today wouldn't exist in their polished forms. These spaces are essential for turning raw musical ideas into professional recordings that can be enjoyed by audiences worldwide.

# The Evolution of Recording Studios

Recording studios have undergone a significant transformation since their early days. Back then, recording music required bulky, cumbersome equipment and a lot of technical know-how. It was a time when only a few could afford to set up a studio, and even fewer had the skills to operate one.

Fast forward to today, and the landscape has changed dramatically. Technological advancements have made recording studios far more accessible and user-friendly. The rise of digital recording means studios now use computer-based audio workstations. This technology allows for easier editing, mixing, and mastering processes. Thanks to these innovations, aspiring entrepreneurs can set up their own studios with a much smaller budget and less technical expertise than was once necessary.

## The Benefits of Starting a Recording Studio Business

There are numerous advantages to starting your own recording studio business. First and foremost, it allows you to turn your passion for music into a profitable venture. How amazing is that? Doing what you love and making money from it!

Moreover, a recording studio offers artists a platform to record and produce their music, contributing significantly to the growth of the local music scene. It's not just about the artists either; a successful recording studio can provide you with a steady stream of income and the potential for expansion as your reputation grows.

## The Challenges and Considerations

Of course, no business venture is without its challenges, and the recording studio business is no exception. The industry is highly competitive, and standing out means offering unique services and exceptional quality. Your studio needs to become a go-to place for artists, which requires a combination of top-notch equipment, skilled personnel, and an inviting atmosphere.

The initial investment for acquiring equipment and setting up a studio can be significant. High-quality microphones, soundproofing materials, mixing consoles, and digital audio workstations don't come cheap. Additionally, understanding market demand, targeting the right audience, and developing strong marketing strategies are crucial to your studio's success.

Staying updated with the latest audio recording technology and trends is also essential. The music industry is always evolving, and to provide the best services to your clients, you need to keep pace with these changes.

## Looking Ahead

In the following chapters, we will dive deeper into various aspects of starting and running a recording studio business. You will learn how to assess your skills and resources, understand your target market, develop your services and pricing, set up your studio and equipment, and navigate the legal and business considerations.

We'll also cover how to implement effective marketing and promotion strategies, acquire clients, provide exceptional service and quality, and ultimately grow your recording studio business. By the end of this guide, you will have a comprehensive understanding of the recording studio business and be well-equipped with the knowledge and tools to start and run your own successful recording studio.

So, are you ready to embark on this exciting journey? Let's dive in and explore the fascinating world of recording studios together!

# Chapter 2: Assessing Your Skills and Resources

Embarking on the journey of starting your own recording studio business is an exciting venture, but it requires careful assessment of your skills and resources. This chapter will guide you through evaluating your expertise, talents, and available resources to ensure you're fully prepared for this rewarding journey.

## Evaluating Your Skills

Before you dive headfirst into the recording studio business, take a moment to evaluate your skills in audio engineering and production. Ask yourself: Do you have experience in recording, mixing, and mastering music? Are you proficient with industry-standard recording software and equipment?

Understanding your technical aptitude is crucial. It helps you pinpoint any areas where you might need improvement. If you find gaps in your knowledge or experience, don't worry. Consider enrolling in audio engineering courses or seeking mentorship from seasoned professionals. Building a strong foundation of knowledge and skills will not only boost your confidence but also reassure potential clients of your expertise.

## Assessing Your Equipment and Resources

Beyond skills, it's essential to evaluate the equipment and resources at your disposal. Start by taking an inventory of your current recording gear. This includes microphones, studio monitors, audio interfaces, and mixing consoles. Assess the quality and capability of your equipment. Does it meet industry standards, or do you need to make upgrades or additional purchases?

Next, consider the space you have available for your studio setup. Is it acoustically treated? Does it provide enough room for musicians and equipment? If your current space is lacking, you might need to explore options like renting a commercial space or building a custom studio to meet your needs.

Financial resources are another critical factor. Starting a recording studio can be capital-intensive. Calculate the funds you have available for initial setup costs, including equipment purchases, studio construction or renovation, and marketing expenses. If you find you need additional funding, research potential sources such as loans, grants, or investors.

## Identifying Your Strengths and Weaknesses

Assessing your skills and resources also means identifying your strengths and weaknesses as a business owner. Are you organized and detail-oriented? Do you have excellent communication and customer service skills? Recognizing your strengths can help you leverage them to attract and retain clients.

Conversely, identifying your weaknesses allows you to address them proactively. For instance, if you lack marketing knowledge, consider investing time in learning about marketing or hiring a marketing expert to ensure effective promotion of your services. Being aware of your limitations and seeking the necessary help will contribute significantly to the success of your recording studio business.

## Conclusion

Assessing your skills and resources is a vital step in starting a recording studio business. By evaluating your expertise, equipment, and financial resources, you can determine your readiness and identify any areas that need improvement or investment. Remember to also consider your strengths and weaknesses as a business owner. Taking actions to enhance your strengths and address your weaknesses will lay a solid foundation for a successful recording studio venture.

# Chapter 3: Understanding Your Target Market

Let's dive into the heart of your recording studio business: identifying and understanding your target market. This is crucial for your success because knowing who your potential clients are and what they need allows you to tailor your services and marketing efforts to meet their specific demands. When you focus on your target market, you can allocate your resources more effectively and significantly boost your chances of attracting the right clients.

## Researching and Defining Your Target Market

To kick off your journey in understanding your target market, you need to conduct thorough research. Start by pinpointing the type of clients who are most likely to use your recording studio services. Think about factors such as their age, musical genre preferences, skill levels, and budget constraints.

It's essential to keep an eye on current music trends and the demand for different types of recording services. This kind of insight helps you spot any gaps in the market and potential niches that you can target. For instance, there might be an emerging trend in indie rock bands looking for affordable studio time or a surge in demand for high-quality podcast recording services.

Don't forget to study your competitors and their clientele. This can provide valuable insights into your own target market. Understanding who your competitors are serving can reveal opportunities for you to differentiate your services and capture a unique segment of the market.

Once you've gathered enough information, it's time to define your target market by creating buyer personas. A buyer persona is a semi-fictional representation of your ideal client. It includes details like demographic information, interests, goals, and pain points. By developing these personas, you'll gain a deeper understanding of your clients, which will help you tailor your marketing messages and services to meet their specific needs.

## Meeting Your Target Market's Needs

Now that you've defined your target market, the next step is to ensure your services align with their specific needs. Think about the types of recording services your target market requires and the level of expertise they expect. This could range from vocal and instrument recording to mixing, mastering, and even music production assistance.

It's also crucial to understand the challenges and pain points your target market might face. If you can offer solutions to their problems, you'll become more valuable to them. For example, if your target market consists of independent musicians on a tight budget, consider offering package deals or discounts to accommodate their financial limitations. Maybe they need flexible recording hours because they're balancing music with a day job—if you can provide that flexibility, you'll stand out.

## Marketing to Your Target Market

To effectively reach your target market, you need a targeted marketing strategy. Use the information you've gathered about your target market to identify the most effective marketing channels. This might include digital platforms like social media, music streaming websites, and online forums where your target audience is likely to be active.

Create compelling and tailored marketing messages that resonate with your target market. Highlight the benefits they'll gain from using your recording studio services. Share testimonials or success stories from previous clients who belong to the same demographic—this builds trust and credibility.

Consider collaborating with local musicians or music influencers who have a following within your target market. This can help amplify your reach and attract potential clients who trust and resonate with these influencers. If a popular local band or a well-known music blogger endorses your studio, their followers are more likely to check you out.

# In Conclusion

Understanding your target market is fundamental to the success of your recording studio business. By conducting thorough research, defining your target market, and aligning your services and marketing efforts with their needs, you can effectively attract and serve the right clients. Always remember to reassess your target market regularly as the music industry evolves. Staying relevant and adaptable will ensure you continue to meet your clients' changing needs and keep your business thriving.

# Chapter 4: Developing Your Services and Pricing

Creating a successful recording studio business isn't just about having top-notch equipment and a cool space. It's about offering a range of services that your target market truly needs and values. Plus, getting your pricing right is crucial to ensure you stay profitable and competitive. Let's dive into how you can develop your services and set your pricing strategy to set your recording studio up for success.

## 1. Understanding Your Target Market's Needs

First things first, you need to really understand what your target market wants. This means doing your homework. Conduct market research and take a good look at what your competitors are offering. What services are they providing? What seems to be popular? Gathering this kind of information is essential.

But don't stop there. Get direct feedback from potential clients. Surveys and focus groups can be incredibly valuable. Ask your target audience what they expect from a recording studio, what services they've used in the past, and what they wish was available. This hands-on approach can give you a much clearer picture of what your market needs.

## 2. Identifying Service Offerings

With a solid understanding of your market, you can start identifying the specific services you'll offer. Think about the various types of recording services that might be in demand. This could include:

- **Album Production:** Helping artists produce full albums from start to finish.
- **Voice-Over Recording:** Providing a space for voice actors to record for ads, animations, etc.
- **Mixing and Mastering:** Fine-tuning recordings to achieve the best possible sound.
- **Live Session Recordings:** Capturing live performances in a studio setting.

Reflect on your own skills and resources as well. What are you and your team best equipped to deliver? This is where your unique strengths come into play.

### 2.1 Specialization

Another strategy is to specialize in a particular niche or genre. Maybe you focus on high-quality recordings for rock bands or become known for producing hip-hop tracks. Specialization can set you apart from the competition and help you build a reputation as an expert in that specific area. Clients often seek out studios that cater specifically to their style or needs.

# 3. Pricing Strategy

Now, let's talk about pricing. Getting your pricing strategy right is key to your financial success. Here are a few things to consider:

## 3.1 Cost Analysis

Start by evaluating your costs. This includes everything from rent and equipment maintenance to utilities and employee salaries. You need to know the minimum amount you need to charge just to cover your expenses. Be sure to factor in both fixed costs (like rent) and variable costs (like utilities) to ensure your pricing is sustainable.

## 3.2 Competitive Analysis

Next, take a look at what your competitors are charging. Understanding market rates for recording studio services can help you set prices that are competitive yet fair. However, be cautious about underpricing your services. Offering your services too cheaply can devalue your expertise and attract clients who are only looking for a bargain, not necessarily quality.

## 3.3 Value-Based Pricing

Consider a value-based pricing approach. This means setting your prices based on the unique value you offer. Think about the quality of your equipment, the experience and expertise of your staff, and the overall reputation of your studio. If you provide a premium service, your pricing should reflect that. Clients often associate higher prices with higher quality, so don't be afraid to position yourself as a premium provider.

# 4. Packaging and Add-On Services

To enhance your offering, think about creating packages or add-on services. This could include:

- **Additional Studio Time:** Offer clients the option to purchase extra hours at a discounted rate.
- **Mixing and Mastering Services:** Include these as part of a package deal.
- **Promotional Support:** Help clients with the promotion of their recordings, which can be a great value-add.

These packages not only increase your revenue potential but also provide a more comprehensive solution for your clients.

# 5. Regularly Review and Adjust

Once you've set up your services and pricing, remember that this isn't a one-and-done task. Regularly review and adjust your offerings and pricing based on market trends and the changing needs of your target market. Stay on top of industry developments and technological advancements that might require you to update your services. Periodically evaluate your pricing to ensure it remains competitive and profitable.

By carefully developing your services and pricing strategy, you can position your recording studio business for success in a competitive market. Take the time to understand your target market, identify valuable service offerings, and determine competitive and sustainable pricing. Fine-tuning these aspects will help you attract and retain clients while maintaining profitability.

# Chapter 5: Setting Up Your Studio and Equipment

Setting up your recording studio and acquiring the necessary equipment is a pivotal step in launching your recording studio business. A well-equipped and thoughtfully arranged studio not only elevates the quality of your recordings but also attracts and retains clients. In this chapter, we will delve into the key components and considerations for setting up your studio to ensure optimal functionality and efficiency.

## Designing Your Studio Space

Before you start purchasing equipment, it's crucial to design your studio space. The layout and acoustics of your studio significantly impact the quality of your recordings. Here are some essential factors to consider when designing your studio space:

### Room Size and Shape:

The size and shape of your studio space play a critical role in its acoustics and sound quality. Ideally, your studio should be spacious enough to accommodate equipment, musicians, and sound isolation measures. Rectangular or square-shaped rooms generally offer better acoustics compared to irregularly shaped rooms.

### Soundproofing and Acoustic Treatment:

To minimize external noise and achieve optimal sound quality, invest in soundproofing and acoustic treatment. This includes installing soundproof doors and windows, adding acoustic panels or diffusers on the walls, and using bass traps in corners to manage low-frequency sounds. Effective soundproofing not only enhances recording quality but also ensures that your sessions don't disturb others.

### Furniture and Ergonomics:

Choose furniture that enhances comfort and ergonomics for you and your clients. Consider investing in adjustable studio desks, comfortable seating, and proper lighting to create a productive and comfortable working environment. Ergonomic furniture can prevent fatigue during long sessions and improve overall efficiency.

## Essential Equipment for Recording Studios

Acquiring the right equipment is crucial for running a successful recording studio business. While the specific equipment you need will depend on your target market and services offered, here are the essential components:

### Microphones:

Invest in a range of high-quality microphones to capture vocals, instruments, and other audio sources. Consider condenser microphones for capturing vocals and acoustic instruments and dynamic microphones for amplifiers and drums. The right microphones can make a significant difference in the clarity and quality of your recordings.

## Audio Interfaces:

An audio interface is the connection between your computer and other audio equipment. Choose an audio interface that fits your needs in terms of input and output channels, sample rate, and connectivity options. A good audio interface ensures that the audio signal is accurately captured and transmitted to your recording software.

## Studio Monitors:

Studio monitors are essential for accurately monitoring your audio recordings. Invest in a pair of high-quality studio monitors that provide a flat and accurate sound representation. Accurate monitoring allows you to make precise adjustments during mixing and mastering.

## Headphones:

Good-quality headphones are necessary for detailed audio monitoring, especially during tracking and mixing sessions. Look for headphones with a wide frequency response and high fidelity. They are invaluable for critical listening and ensuring that your mixes translate well across different playback systems.

### Computer and Recording Software:

A reliable computer and recording software are essential for audio recording, editing, and mixing. Choose a computer with enough processing power and storage capacity to handle your projects, and select recording software that suits your workflow and preferences. Popular recording software includes Pro Tools, Logic Pro, and Ableton Live.

### Outboard Gear:

Consider investing in outboard gear such as preamps, compressors, equalizers, and effects processors to add color and character to your recordings. Carefully choose gear that complements your recording style and target market's preferences. Outboard gear can provide unique sound qualities that digital plugins may not replicate.

## Setting Up Your Studio

Once you have acquired the necessary equipment, it's time to set up your studio. Follow these steps to ensure a smooth and efficient setup process:

### Cable Management:

Organize and label your cables to minimize clutter and ensure easy troubleshooting. Use cable ties and cable management systems to keep cables organized and prevent tripping hazards. Good cable management not only looks professional but also simplifies maintenance and setup changes.

## Equipment Placement:

Strategically place your equipment to optimize workflow and minimize interference. Keep sensitive equipment away from potential sources of electrical interference. Consider investing in racks or studio furniture to keep your equipment organized and easily accessible. Proper placement ensures that your workflow is smooth and efficient.

## Calibration and Testing:

Once everything is set up, calibrate your monitors, headphones, and audio interfaces to ensure accurate audio reproduction. Conduct thorough testing to ensure all equipment is functioning properly and troubleshoot any issues that may arise. Calibration is essential for maintaining the integrity of your recordings.

## User Guidelines:

Create user guidelines and standard operating procedures for your studio to ensure consistency and efficiency. This includes guidelines for equipment use, session setup, and file management. Clear guidelines help maintain a professional environment and ensure that everyone using the studio knows the proper protocols.

By carefully designing your studio space, acquiring essential equipment, and setting up your studio with efficiency in mind, you will create an environment that supports high-quality recordings and enhances the overall client experience. Take the time to research and invest in the right equipment for your specific needs, and keep your studio organized and well-maintained.

Embarking on this journey with a well-thought-out plan and the right tools will set you up for success, allowing your recording studio business to flourish and thrive.

# Chapter 6: Legal and Business Considerations

Running a successful recording studio business requires more than just technical skills and equipment. It also involves understanding and addressing the legal and business aspects of the industry. In this chapter, we will explore the important considerations you need to keep in mind to ensure compliance with regulations and protect your business interests.

## Legal Structure

When you're starting your recording studio business, one of the first steps is to choose the right legal structure. This decision is crucial as it affects everything from how you file taxes to your personal liability. The most common options include sole proprietorship, partnership, limited liability company (LLC), and corporation.

Each legal structure comes with its own set of benefits and drawbacks. For instance, a sole proprietorship is easy to set up and gives you complete control, but it also means you're personally liable for any business debts. On the other hand, forming an LLC or corporation can provide liability protection, but these structures can be more complex and costly to establish. To make the best choice, consult with a legal professional who can help you determine the most suitable structure for your specific situation.

## Licenses and Permits

Operating a recording studio business may require obtaining various licenses and permits, and these requirements can vary widely depending on your location and the services you offer. Some common licenses and permits to consider include:

- **Business License**: This is a basic requirement for any business operation, so be sure to check with your local government to understand the process.
- **Music Licensing**: If you plan to offer recording or production services that involve copyrighted music, you may need to obtain licenses from organizations like ASCAP, BMI, or SESAC.
- **Noise Permits**: Depending on your location, you may need permits to ensure compliance with noise regulations. This is particularly important if your studio is in a residential area.
- **Zoning Permits**: Make sure your studio location is zoned for commercial use. If it's not, you may need to apply for a special permit or find a suitable location where commercial activities are allowed.

## Contracts and Agreements

Creating clear and comprehensive contracts and agreements is crucial in the recording studio business. Some important contracts to consider include:

- **Recording Contracts**: These agreements outline the terms and conditions between you and the artist or band. They typically include details such as rights, royalties, payment terms, and project timelines.
- **Client Agreements**: These contracts specify the scope of work, payment terms, and any additional services or terms not covered in the recording contract.
- **Collaboration Agreements**: If you collaborate with other professionals, such as session musicians or producers, it's important to have agreements in place that outline the terms and conditions of the collaboration.

## Copyright and Intellectual Property

As a recording studio owner, understanding copyright and intellectual property laws is essential. Make sure you are aware of the rights and responsibilities associated with recording, producing, and distributing copyrighted material. Additionally, consider registering your own musical works and recordings with the appropriate copyright organizations to protect your intellectual property.

## Insurance

Protecting your studio and equipment with the right insurance coverage is essential. Consider obtaining the following types of insurance:

- **General Liability Insurance**: This protects your business from claims related to property damage, bodily injury, and advertising claims.
- **Equipment Insurance**: This covers the cost of repairing or replacing damaged or stolen equipment.
- **Professional Liability Insurance**: Also known as errors and omissions (E&O) insurance, this protects you from claims alleging negligence or mistakes in your services.

## Accounting and Taxes

Keeping accurate financial records and understanding your tax obligations are important for the success of your recording studio business. Consider hiring a professional accountant or using accounting software to track your income and expenses effectively. Additionally, consult with a tax professional to ensure compliance with tax regulations and take advantage of any tax deductions or credits available to your business.

## Data Protection and Privacy

Given the sensitive nature of the data you may be handling, such as client recordings and personal information, it's essential to have measures in place to protect data and ensure privacy. Implement secure data storage and backup systems, use encryption protocols when transferring data, and have a privacy policy in place that outlines how you handle and protect client information.

## Conclusion

Understanding and addressing the legal and business considerations in the recording studio industry are crucial for the long-term success of your business. By taking the time to choose the right legal structure, obtain necessary licenses and permits, create solid contracts and agreements, protect your intellectual property, and ensure adequate insurance coverage, you can minimize risks and create a solid foundation for your recording studio business.

# Chapter 7: Marketing and Promotion Strategies

Let's dive into the world of marketing and promotion, which are essential for the success of any business, including your recording studio. Effective marketing will help you connect with your target market, build brand awareness, attract clients, and ultimately grow your business. In this chapter, we'll explore various strategies to effectively market and promote your recording studio.

## Utilize the Power of Social Media

Social media platforms have revolutionized the way businesses connect with their audience and promote their services. As a recording studio owner, you can harness the power of social media platforms like Facebook, Instagram, Twitter, and LinkedIn to showcase your studio, share updates, and engage with potential clients.

Start by creating a professional social media presence for your recording studio. Set up dedicated profiles and pages that reflect the identity and ethos of your business. Share high-quality photos and videos of your studio space, equipment, and previous projects to give potential clients a glimpse of what you offer. Highlight the success stories of your clients and their positive experiences at your studio.

Engagement is key on social media. Regularly post content related to music production, recording tips, and industry news to keep your audience informed and interested. Encourage your clients to share their experiences of working with your studio on their social media and to tag your business in their posts.

Consider running targeted social media ads to reach a wider audience. These platforms allow you to set specific parameters such as location, age, musical interests, and budget, ensuring your ads reach your ideal clients.

## Create a Professional Website

A professional website is the cornerstone of your online presence. It's where potential clients will go to learn more about your services, browse your portfolio, and get in touch with you.

Ensure your website is visually appealing, user-friendly, and optimized for mobile devices. Clearly showcase your services, pricing options, and testimonials from satisfied clients. Make it easy for potential clients to contact you by providing a dedicated contact form or booking system.

Adding a blog section to your website can be incredibly beneficial. Regularly share valuable content related to music production, recording techniques, and industry insights. This will not only attract organic traffic to your website but also position you as an expert in your field.

## Collaborate with Local Musicians and Influencers

Networking and collaborations are powerful marketing tools. Reach out to local musicians, bands, and influencers in your area and explore opportunities for collaboration. Offer free or discounted recording sessions to talented up-and-coming artists in exchange for exposure and promotion.

Collaborate with influencers who have a strong following on social media or run a popular music blog. Their endorsement can showcase your studio and services to a wider audience. Attend local music events, open mic nights, and industry conferences to meet new musicians and industry professionals. Building meaningful relationships and generating word-of-mouth referrals can be invaluable for the growth of your recording studio business.

## Offer Special Promotions and Referral Incentives

To attract new clients and encourage repeat business, consider offering special promotions and referral incentives. For instance, you could offer discounted rates for first-time clients or bundle recording and mixing services at a discounted package price.

Implement a referral program where you reward your existing clients for referring new clients to your studio. This could be in the form of discounts, free recording hours, or exclusive perks. Word-of-mouth recommendations can be a powerful marketing tool, and incentivizing referrals can help ensure your clients are actively promoting your business.

## Monitor and Analyze Your Marketing Efforts

To determine the effectiveness of your marketing and promotion strategies, it's crucial to monitor and analyze your efforts. Track key metrics such as website traffic, social media engagement, and conversion rates to gain insights into what is working and what needs improvement.

Use analytics tools and platforms to gather data on user behavior, demographics, and preferences. This data will help you refine your marketing strategies and make informed decisions on where to allocate your resources. Regularly revisit your marketing plan and adjust your strategies based on your findings.

Stay updated with the latest trends in marketing and continue to experiment with new platforms and techniques to stay ahead of the competition.

By implementing these marketing and promotion strategies, you can effectively reach your target market, attract clients, and grow your recording studio business. Stay consistent with your efforts, provide exceptional service, and showcase your passion for music production to differentiate yourself in the industry.

# Chapter 8: Acquiring Clients and Building Relationships

Running a successful recording studio business hinges on a crucial aspect: acquiring clients. To grow your business and maximize profits, you need a steady stream of clients booking your services. Let's explore some effective strategies to help you acquire new clients and build lasting relationships with them.

## Developing a Client Acquisition Strategy

Acquiring clients isn't just about waiting for them to find you; it's about actively seeking them out and presenting your studio as the best option. Here are some ways to attract new clients:

### 1. Build a Strong Online Presence

In today's digital age, having a robust online presence is essential. Start by creating a professional website that showcases your services, portfolio, and testimonials. Make sure your website is optimized for search engines so potential clients can easily find you.

But don't stop at just a website. Dive into social media. Create dedicated profiles for your recording studio on platforms like Facebook, Instagram, and LinkedIn. Regularly share high-quality content that highlights your expertise and the services you offer. Engage with your audience by responding to comments and messages promptly. This interaction helps build a community around your brand and keeps your studio top-of-mind for potential clients.

## 2. Network with Industry Professionals

Networking is a powerful tool in the music industry. Attend local music events, conferences, and workshops to meet musicians, producers, and other industry professionals. Engage in conversations, exchange contact information, and establish a rapport with these individuals.

Consider collaborating with local musicians and influencers. Offer discounted or free recording sessions to up-and-coming artists or seek partnerships with established musicians. These collaborations can expand your reach and bring in new clients. Building these relationships not only gains you exposure but also creates potential long-term partnerships.

## 3. Leverage Word-of-Mouth Marketing

Word-of-mouth marketing is incredibly effective. Provide exceptional service to your existing clients and encourage them to share their positive experiences with others. Offer referral incentives, such as discounts or additional services, to clients who refer new business to you.

Collect testimonials and reviews from satisfied clients and prominently display them on your website and social media platforms. Positive reviews and testimonials significantly boost your credibility and attract new clients.

# Building Long-Term Relationships with Clients

Acquiring clients is just the beginning. Building long-term relationships with them is crucial for the ongoing success of your recording studio business. Here's how you can foster strong client relationships:

## 1. Provide Exceptional Customer Service

Delivering exceptional customer service is key. Be responsive to inquiries and address any concerns promptly. Clear and effective communication is essential, and always strive to exceed your clients' expectations. Creating a welcoming and comfortable environment in your studio can significantly enhance the client experience.

## 2. Tailor Services to Meet Their Needs

Every client is unique with different needs and preferences. Take the time to understand their specific requirements and tailor your services accordingly. Offer personalized recommendations and solutions that align with their musical goals and vision. This customized approach makes clients feel valued and understood.

## 3. Regularly Communicate and Follow Up

Maintain regular communication with your clients, even after their recording sessions are complete.

Send follow-up emails or make courtesy calls to check on their progress and offer additional support or services. This shows your commitment to their success and reinforces their trust in your studio.

## 4. Offer Loyalty Programs and Incentives

Reward client loyalty by implementing a loyalty program or offering incentives for repeat bookings. This could include discounts on future services, exclusive access to special events, or priority scheduling. Creating a sense of exclusivity and value for your loyal clients will encourage them to continue working with you and refer others to your studio.

## 5. Continuously Seek Feedback

Regularly seek feedback from your clients to ensure their satisfaction and identify areas for improvement. Provide opportunities for them to voice their opinions and make suggestions. Demonstrating that you value their feedback and are committed to their satisfaction will foster stronger client relationships.

Remember, acquiring clients and building relationships is an ongoing process. Continuously evaluate and adjust your client acquisition and relationship-building strategies to meet the evolving needs of your target market. By consistently delivering exceptional service and fostering strong client relationships, you'll position your recording studio business for long-term success.

# Chapter 9: Providing Exceptional Service and Quality

Delivering exceptional service and maintaining high-quality standards are paramount to the success and reputation of your recording studio business. When clients have a memorable experience, they are more likely to return and spread positive word-of-mouth recommendations. In this chapter, we'll dive into various strategies and best practices to ensure you consistently provide top-notch service and quality in your recording studio.

## Understanding Client Expectations

To provide exceptional service, it's essential to understand what your clients expect and need. Communication is key here. Start by having a detailed conversation with your clients before any recording session. Discuss their project goals, the sound they're aiming for, and any specific requirements they might have. By doing this, you can tailor your services to meet their unique needs and deliver a personalized experience.

## Creating a Welcoming Atmosphere

The atmosphere of your recording studio significantly impacts the overall client experience. Ensure your studio is always clean, organized, and well-maintained. Create a comfortable and inviting environment where clients feel relaxed and inspired to create. Pay attention to the small details like lighting, temperature, and decor to craft a welcoming atmosphere that fosters creativity and comfort.

Imagine walking into a studio that feels more like a cluttered basement than a creative haven. It wouldn't set the right tone for a productive session. Conversely, a well-thought-out space can help artists feel at home, encouraging their best performances.

## Providing Expertise and Guidance

As the owner of a recording studio, you're not just offering a space but also your expertise in audio engineering and production. Use your knowledge to guide your clients throughout their recording process. Offer suggestions that can enhance their recordings and provide constructive feedback to help them overcome any challenges. By positioning yourself as a knowledgeable and supportive partner in their music-making journey, you build trust and respect.

Think of it this way: you're not just pressing record. You're helping to shape their sound and bring their vision to life. Your insights can make a significant difference in the final product.

## Ensuring Technical Excellence

Technical excellence is a cornerstone of exceptional service in a recording studio. Make sure all your equipment is well-maintained and regularly calibrated for optimal performance. Stay updated with the latest advancements in recording technology and proficiently use the software and hardware tools available in your studio. This ensures you deliver high-quality recordings that meet industry standards.

Nothing frustrates a client more than technical glitches during a session. By keeping your equipment in top shape and staying on top of new technologies, you can avoid these pitfalls and ensure a smooth recording experience.

## Delivering Timely and Effective Results

Meeting deadlines and delivering results on time is crucial for maintaining a good reputation. Efficient time management and resource allocation are essential. Communicate clearly with clients about project timelines and provide regular updates on their progress. Consistently delivering on time builds trust and reliability with your clients.

Imagine telling a client their project will be ready in a week and then taking a month. It can tarnish your reputation. On the other hand, consistently meeting deadlines shows professionalism and reliability.

## Acknowledging and Resolving Issues

Even with the best intentions, issues can arise during recording sessions or post-production. It's vital to address these issues promptly and professionally. Listen actively to your clients' concerns and work together to find solutions.

Whether it's technical difficulties or creative differences, maintaining open communication and a problem-solving mindset can help you navigate challenges and ensure client satisfaction.

Issues are inevitable, but how you handle them can make or break your client's experience. By addressing problems quickly and effectively, you show your commitment to their satisfaction.

## Soliciting and Acting on Feedback

Continuous improvement is key to providing exceptional service. Encourage your clients to share their thoughts and suggestions after each recording session. Pay close attention to both positive feedback and constructive criticism. Implement necessary adjustments based on the feedback you receive. This not only helps you improve but also demonstrates your commitment to client satisfaction.

Feedback is a gift. By actively seeking and acting on it, you show clients that their opinions matter and that you're dedicated to continually enhancing your services.

## Conclusion

Providing exceptional service and quality in your recording studio business sets you apart from the competition and helps build a loyal client base. By understanding client expectations, creating a welcoming atmosphere, providing expertise and guidance, ensuring technical excellence, delivering timely results, addressing issues professionally, and actively seeking feedback, you can consistently exceed client expectations.

Remember, every interaction with your clients is an opportunity to showcase your commitment to excellence. Creating a memorable experience for them will not only make them repeat customers but also turn them into ambassadors for your studio. Keep striving for the highest standards, and your recording studio will become a go-to destination for exceptional service and quality.

# Chapter 10: Growing Your Recording Studio Business

Congratulations! You've successfully established your recording studio business. Now, it's time to shift your focus to growth and expansion. This chapter will guide you through various strategies and techniques to scale your business and reach new heights.

## Investing in Marketing and Advertising

One of the key elements to growing your recording studio business is to invest in marketing and advertising. By increasing your brand visibility and reaching a wider audience, you can attract more clients and expand your client base. Utilize both online and offline marketing channels to promote your services. Here are some effective strategies to consider:

### Online Marketing

- **Enhance Your Online Presence**: Continuously update and optimize your website to showcase your services, portfolio, and client testimonials. Ensure your website is easy to navigate, mobile-friendly, and optimized for search engines.

- **Content Marketing**: Start a blog on your website and provide valuable content related to the music industry and recording studio services. Share tips, industry insights, and current trends. This will position you as an expert and attract organic traffic to your website.
- **Email Marketing**: Build an email list of existing and potential clients. Send regular newsletters with updates, promotions, and valuable content. Segment your email list and personalize the emails to enhance engagement.
- **Social Media Marketing**: Utilize popular social media platforms such as Facebook, Instagram, Twitter, and YouTube to connect with your target audience. Create engaging content, share studio updates, client testimonials, behind-the-scenes videos, and collaborate with local musicians and influencers.
- **Paid Advertising**: Consider running targeted online ads, such as Google AdWords or social media ads, to reach a wider audience. Set specific goals and budgets for your ad campaigns and track their performance to optimize results.

## Offline Marketing

- **Local Networking**: Attend local music events, industry conferences, and join music associations to network with potential clients and industry professionals. Building relationships can lead to collaboration opportunities.

- **Traditional Advertising**: Explore options for traditional advertising, such as print ads in local music magazines or newspapers. Advertise on local radio stations or sponsor community events to increase brand awareness.

## Expanding Your Services

To grow your recording studio business, consider expanding your services to cater to a wider range of clients and meet their evolving needs. Here are a few ideas to explore:

- **Offer Additional Production Services**: Besides providing recording services, consider offering mixing, mastering, and audio production services. This will enable you to cater to clients who require a complete package.
- **Provide Remote Recording Options**: With advancements in technology, remote recording has become a popular choice for many artists. Invest in the necessary equipment and software to offer remote recording options for clients who cannot physically visit your studio.
- **Collaborate with Other Professionals**: Build relationships with musicians, producers, and songwriters to offer collaborative services. This can include songwriting and production sessions where clients can work with experienced professionals to enhance their music.
- **Licensing and Synchronization**: Explore opportunities to license music for TV, film,

commercials, and other media platforms. This can provide an additional revenue stream for your recording studio business.

## Customer Retention and Referrals

One of the most effective ways to grow your recording studio business is through customer retention and referrals. Happy clients not only become repeat customers but also act as brand ambassadors, recommending your services to their network. Here are some strategies to ensure customer satisfaction and generate referrals:

- **Exceptional Customer Service**: Continue providing exceptional service by understanding and meeting your clients' expectations. Respond promptly to their inquiries, be flexible with scheduling, and go the extra mile to ensure their satisfaction.
- **Loyalty Programs and Incentives**: Implement loyalty programs to reward frequent clients. Offer special discounts or incentives for repeat bookings. This will encourage clients to continue using your services and refer others.
- **Referral Programs**: Create a referral program where clients receive incentives for referring new clients to your recording studio. Offer discounts, free sessions, or other rewards to show appreciation for their support.
- **Request Testimonials and Reviews**: Ask satisfied clients to provide testimonials and reviews that you can showcase on your website and social media platforms. Positive

feedback acts as social proof and attracts new clients.

## Continuously Evolving and Adapting

Lastly, to ensure the long-term growth and success of your recording studio business, it's essential to continuously evolve and adapt to the changing industry landscape. Stay updated with the latest trends, advancements in technology, and shifts in client

preferences. Regularly reassess your strategies, services, and pricing to remain competitive in the market. Seek feedback from your clients and analyze data to identify areas for improvement. By staying proactive and continuously innovating, you will position your recording studio business for sustainable growth.

## Conclusion

Growing your recording studio business requires a multi-faceted approach. You need to be proactive in your marketing strategies, expand your service offerings, focus on customer retention and referrals, and continuously evolve to meet industry demands. By implementing these strategies, you will be able to establish yourself as a prominent player in the music industry and achieve long-term success with your recording studio business.